# What is
# smell?

## Molly Aloian

🌳 Crabtree Publishing Company

www.crabtreebooks.com

**Author**
Molly Aloian

**Publishing plan research and development**
Sean Charlebois, Reagan Miller
Crabtree Publishing Company

**Editorial director**
Kathy Middleton

**Editor**
Crystal Sikkens

**Proofreader**
Kelly McNiven

**Design**
Samara Parent
Margaret Amy Salter

**Photo research**
Samara Parent

**Production coordinator and prepress technician**
Margaret Amy Salter

**Print coordinator**
Katherine Berti

**Photographs**
Dreamstime: page 13
Thinkstock: cover (center), page 1 (milk carton)
All other images by Shutterstock

**Library and Archives Canada Cataloguing in Publication**

Aloian, Molly
    What is smell? / Molly Aloian.

(Senses close-up)
Includes index.
Issued also in electronic format.
ISBN 978-0-7787-0971-8 (bound).--ISBN 978-0-7787-0999-2 (pbk.)

    1. Smell--Juvenile literature. I. Title. II. Series: Senses close-up

QP458.A56 2013      j612.8'6      C2013-901612-0

**Library of Congress Cataloging-in-Publication Data**

Aloian, Molly.
  What is smell? / Molly Aloian.
    pages cm. -- (Senses close-up)
  Audience: 5-8.
  Audience: K to grade 3.
  Includes index.
  ISBN 978-0-7787-0971-8 (reinforced library binding) -- ISBN 978-0-7787-0999-2 (pbk.) -- ISBN 978-1-4271-9293-6 (electronic pdf) -- ISBN 978-1-4271-9217-2 (electronic html)
  1. Smell--Juvenile literature. 2. Nose--Juvenile literature. I. Title.

QP458.A39 2013
612.8'6--dc23
                    2013009066

# Crabtree Publishing Company

www.crabtreebooks.com    1-800-387-7650

Printed in the U.S.A./042013/SX20130306

**Published in Canada**
**Crabtree Publishing**
616 Welland Ave.
St. Catharines, Ontario
L2M 5V6

**Published in the United States**
**Crabtree Publishing**
PMB 59051
350 Fifth Avenue, 59th Floor
New York, New York 10118

**Published in the United Kingdom**
**Crabtree Publishing**
Maritime House
Basin Road North, Hove
BN41 1WR

**Published in Australia**
**Crabtree Publishing**
3 Charles Street
Coburg North
VIC 3058

# Contents

# Your sense of smell

Smell is one of your five main senses. Your other four senses are touch, sight, hearing, and taste. You use your senses every day to help you learn about the world around you.

## Smell it

You smell through your nose. Take a moment to breathe in through your nose and sniff the air around you. What can you smell? You are surrounded by different smells all of the time.

### What do you think?

In what ways do we use our five senses?

5

# Smell and taste

The airway from your nose that you use to breathe is also connected to your mouth. This causes your senses of smell and taste to work together. When you are tasting your food with your tongue you are also breathing in the food's smell with your nose.

*This boy is tasting his ice cream with his sense of taste and smell.*

## Trouble smelling

A lot of what you taste comes from your sense of smell. When you have a cold and your nose is plugged, it can be hard to taste your food. This is because you are not able to breathe in the food's smell through your nose.

If you don't like the taste of something, try pinching your nose.

What do you *think?*

"Sweet" and "sour" describe tastes as well as smells. What foods can you think of that taste and smell sweet or sour?

# Parts of the nose

Your nose is made of bone and **cartilage**. It has two very important jobs. Your nose helps you breathe in air and takes the air to your **lungs**. Your nose also smells. All day long, your nose works together with your brain to smell.

## Nice nostrils

Everything you are smelling is giving off tiny scent **particles**. The particles are too small for you to see. You breathe in these particles with air through your **nostrils**. You have two nostrils at the bottom of your nose.

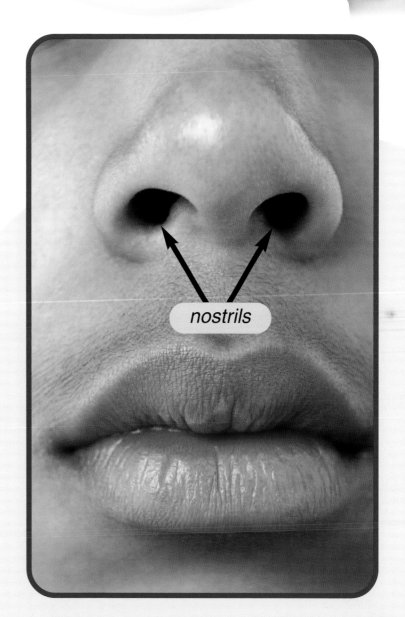

nostrils

# Time to smell

These tiny particles pass through your nostrils and stick to **mucus** inside your nose. There are also special **sensors** inside your nose. They send messages to your brain about the particles in the air.

## Smelling sensors

These messages travel to your brain along thin strings of tissue called **nerves**. Your brain gets the messages and then tells you about what you are smelling.

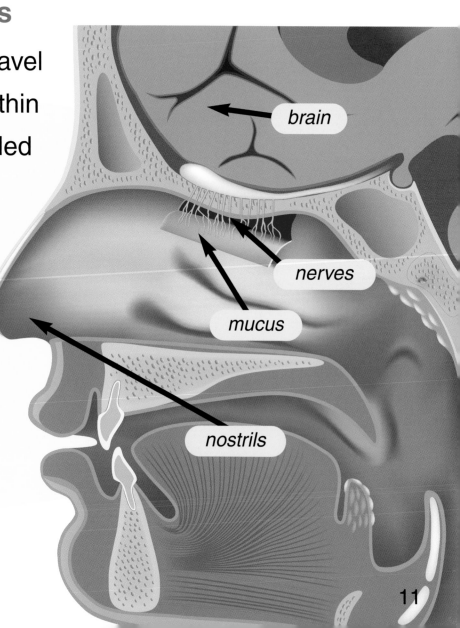

brain

nerves

mucus

nostrils

# Types of smells

There are thousands of types of smells. Some smells, such as cookies baking or sweet-smelling flowers, may smell good to you. Others may smell bad. Your brother's smelly sweat socks may smell bad.

## What do you think?

*What is your favorite smell? Do you like clean smells, such as soap or laundry? Do you like strong smells such as onions? Why or why not?*

## Smells are reminders

Some smells may remind you of people or events. The smell of a certain perfume may remind you of your mother. The smell of freshly cut grass may remind you of summer. The smell of turkey may remind you of Thanksgiving.

# Smelling helps you

Your sense of smell helps you learn about what is going on around you. You can smell your food before you eat it. If a food or drink smells bad, it may be bad to eat or drink.

*The smell of sour milk warns you that the milk is bad.*

## Smelling danger

Some smells can warn you of danger. If you ever smell gas, tell an adult right away. The smell of smoke tells you that there may be a dangerous fire nearby. Cigarette smoke is another dangerous smell.

*If you ever smell smoke in your home, leave the building right away.*

# I can't smell

Most people can smell between 3,000 to 10,000 different **scents**. That's a lot of smells! Some people cannot smell at all. They have no sense of smell. This condition is called **anosmia**.

## Blocked out

If you have a cold, thick mucus usually plugs up your nose. This mucus blocks scent particles from reaching the sensors inside your nose. This makes it hard to smell different scents.

**What do you think?**

*What other sense does not work as well when your sense of smell isn't working?*

# Animals smell, too

Animals can smell, too. In fact, many animals have a better sense of smell than people. A dog can smell things that people cannot smell. A mosquito can smell your scent from up to 100 feet (30 m) away.

*Police dogs can be trained to find scents that people cannot smell. The dogs help police find things that are hidden.*

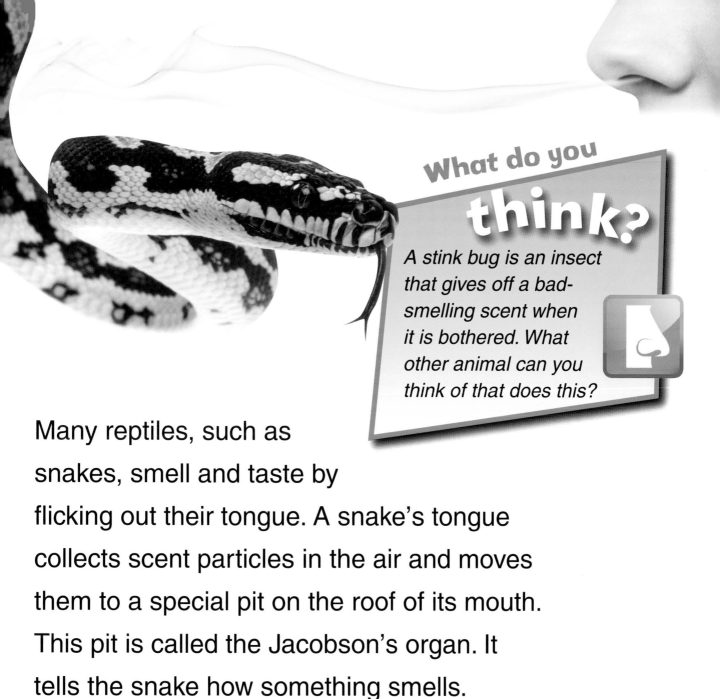

**What do you think?**

A stink bug is an insect that gives off a bad-smelling scent when it is bothered. What other animal can you think of that does this?

Many reptiles, such as snakes, smell and taste by flicking out their tongue. A snake's tongue collects scent particles in the air and moves them to a special pit on the roof of its mouth. This pit is called the Jacobson's organ. It tells the snake how something smells.

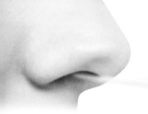

It is important to take care of your sense of smell. Never put things inside your nose. Doing so can damage your sense of smell. When you blow your nose, be gentle. Try to blow one nostril at a time.

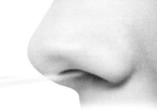

## The nose knows

Keep your nose away from harmful or strong chemicals. Do not smell anything unfamiliar. When you smell something, be sure to **waft**, or gently wave your hand over the top of what you are smelling. This is much safer than taking a huge sniff.

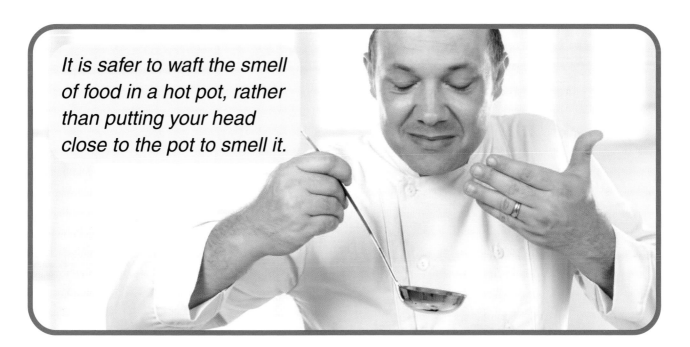

*It is safer to waft the smell of food in a hot pot, rather than putting your head close to the pot to smell it.*

# Smell it!

This activity is a fun way to use your sense of smell.

You will need:

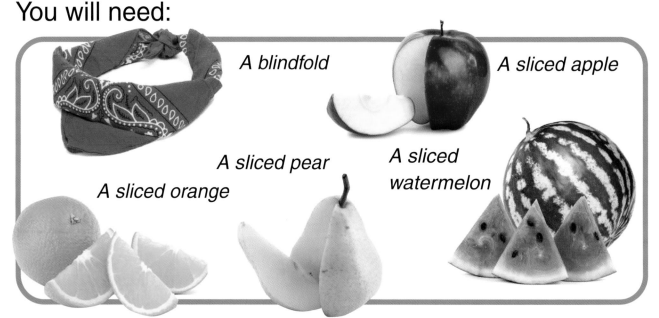

A blindfold

A sliced apple

A sliced pear

A sliced orange

A sliced watermelon

Blindfold a friend and ask your friend to smell each of the fruits.

*Did he or she guess the different fruits correctly?*
*How does not being able to see affect the sense of smell?*
*What other senses could your friend use to help figure out which fruit is which?*

# Learning more

## Books

*What is Smell? (Lightning Bolt Books: Your Amazing Senses)*
by Jennifer Boothroyd. Lerner Publications, 2009.

*Tasting and Smelling (Sparklers Senses)* by Katie Dicker.
M. Evans and Company, 2011.

*Smell It! (Let's Start Science)* by Sally Hewitt.
Crabtree Publishing Company, 2008.

*My Senses Help Me* (My World) by Bobbie Kalman.
Crabtree Publishing Company, 2010.

## Websites

All About Your Senses: Experiments to Try
http://kidshealth.org/kid/closet/experiments/experiment_main.html

Sid the Science Kid
http://pbskids.org/sid/isense.html

The Sense of Smell
www.wisc-online.com/Objects/ViewObject.aspx?ID=AP14004

Your Nose
http://kidshealth.org/kid/htbw/nose.html

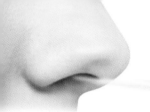

# Words to know

**anosmia** (an-OZ-mee-uh) noun  Loss of the sense of smell

**cartilage** (KAHR-tl-ij) noun  Soft, flexible tissue

**lungs** (luhngz) noun  Organs that we use to breathe

**mucus** (MYOO-kuhs) noun A slippery, sticky substance inside the body

**nerves** (nurvz) noun  Thin strings of tissue; nerves carry messages from your brain to other parts of your body

**nostrils** (NOS-truhlz) noun  The two outer openings of the nose

**particles** (PAHR-ti-kuhlz) noun  Very tiny parts of matter

**scent** (sent) noun  A smell left by something or someone

**sensors** (SEN-sawr) noun  Parts of your body that send messages to your nerves and brain

**waft** (wahft) verb  To move air toward the nose using the hand

*A noun is a person, place, or thing. A verb is an action word that tells you what someone or something does.*

# Index